mixed feelings

abraham rodriguez

central
avenue
PUBLISHING

2022

Published by Central Avenue Publishing, an imprint of Central Avenue Marketing Ltd.
centralavenuepublishing.com
@centavepub

MIXED FEELINGS

Trade Paperback: 978-1-77168-270-1
Ebook: 978-1-77168-271-8

Published in Canada
Printed in United States of America

1. POETRY / Love & Erotica
2. POETRY / American/Hispanic & Latino

10 9 8 7 6 5 4 3 2 1

mixed
feelings

feel with me

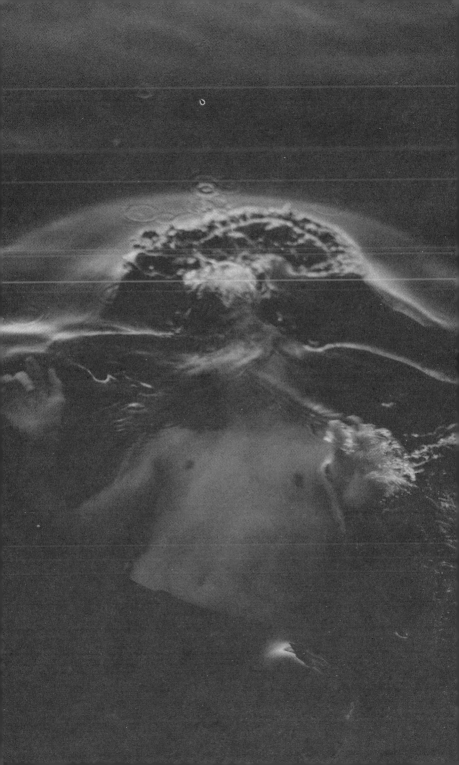

no table of contents

these poems are mixed
throughout the pages of this book
as are my feelings
throughout my
heart
soul
mind
and body

welcome to me
as i hope
you are welcomed
to a new part of you

a part of me
is happy for you

the other part
will never be

that part
will always wish
you were with
me

we lay on my bed

i held you tight in my arms

we let our souls do the talking
  as our lips stayed shut
and our breathing became one

  i knew the feeling was mutual
when you softly said
i feel safe

those three simple words
traveled through my body
  all the way to my heart
where they exploded
and spilled every ounce of my love
making me realize
how strongly i felt the same way

i responded
me too
and waited for those words
  to travel through you
as i held you even tighter
  thinking about
how special you are

your lips
were good at kissing
  but even better at
keeping
every little secret
you knew would
ruin
the dynamic
we established
  upon never
catching feelings

it's time for me
   to go back
to therapy

let's try this once again
let's see if this session
of expensive undivided attention
will be the one that finally
pushes me through
to no longer being in love
with you

   —i need help

it feels so right
but it's so soon

how can i feel this comfortable
without truly knowing you?

i've held you in my arms for seconds
and i already know
i want you in my arms
   for a lifetime more

i hope my name
is the one you get mixed up
and accidentally call
your new love

we sit

you talk

  i listen

or at least i try to

the tension is thick

  the sexual kind

i'm trying to be present but all i can think about

is kissing you

i fight the battle inside my mind

about everything i want to do

to you

i'm trying to listen

i hear your voice

but not your words

as i stare at your lips

wanting, lusting, fantasizing

waiting for you to finish your sentence

then i ask *can i kiss you*

  you respond *of course*

and finally i get what i've been craving

since the moment you walked

through the door

your lips

on mine

—we sit you talk i listen

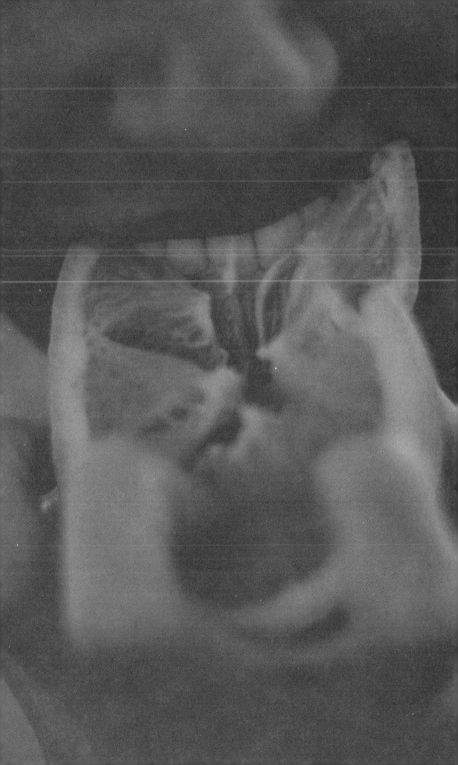

i would never take my eyes off of me
   if i were you

i hope whatever you see
of me, in me
is worth the view

i'm scared
my love
for you
will never
fade away

but would it
really be
so bad
if it stayed?

i just want to sit in my car
with you by my side
while we drink iced coffee
and stare at the night sky
telling each other stories
kissing under the stars
at the top of the hill
with the view of our city
where i found
you

i went all in
at loving you
in the hopes that
it would cause you
  to maybe
love me too

but even
giving you
every bit of me
still wasn't enough
to convince you
i was worth
keeping

i wish
you'd never put that idea
in my head

it's taking over me
every second of every day

i can't escape it
but maybe i don't want to
because i enjoy the thought of it

i'm just scared it won't happen

i don't want to get my hopes up

i don't want to be let down
by you

again

i hide
what i'm afraid
you won't like

to keep you

as much as i believe i'm over you
   still the hardest thing to do
is delete our messages from my phone
   even though i never go back to read them

   a part of me can't let go
of the proof we showed each other
of all the love we had for one another

it scares me

the way i'm in love with you
  before ever meeting
the way i can see us arriving at my parents' house
  and you greeting my family
the way i can feel your warm skin
  pressed against my cheek when i wake in the morning
the way i can see you folding your laundry
  and putting it in my drawer that's now filled with your belongings
the way i can hear you call me *baby*
  when you ask me if i would like a cup of coffee

it scares me
how quick and easy
i throw myself
  into a fantasy about everything
i want us to be
before ever meeting

    —it scares me

my mouth says
all the things
you want to hear
as my heart
sheds a tear

mi amor

toma un momento

respira profundo

cierra tus ojos

imagina tu futuro

si te dejaras amarme

   completamente

ahora dime

¿qué miras?

¿vale la pena?

is it worth it?

what do you see?

now tell me

completely

if you allowed yourself to love me

imagine your future

close your eyes

breathe in deeply

take a moment

my love

i've prayed to god
　to change me
but i'm still
the same

i believe that's god
telling me
i'm supposed to be
this way

you know exactly
   what to say
to make me
   stay

i make sure my place
is sparkling clean
so you can come over
and ruin everything
including me

you get what you want
what you came for
you leave
i clean up
and regret everything

i feel so empty
yet i know
i'll find myself
in this exact same place
   again and again

i need something
to fill me up
even if it's only
temporary

a thousand eyes on me
  and yours
are the only ones
  i seek

my chest
pressed against yours
one arm under you
the other over you
our waists touching
our sacred areas kissing
my legs intertwined with yours

my home position
  the only home
i want to live in

the sight or sound
of that name makes
my face and heart
wrinkle in disgust

the fire in me has been contained for too long
it's now my time to break free and let it burn
stronger and bigger than ever before
with no barriers or do-not-enter zones
burning freely with no extinguishers in sight
  until it burns out and i light
a new fire within me
that's incomparably bright

—wildfire

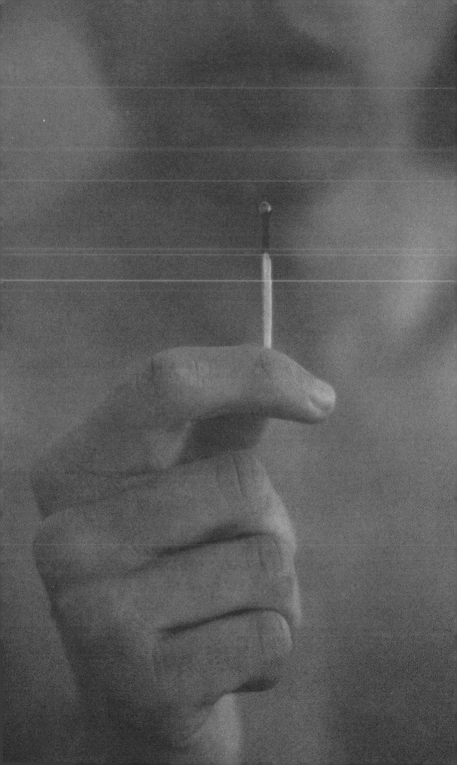

i keep searching
    for love
from you
for me
but it doesn't exist

never did
never will

still i keep searching
    hoping one day
it will appear

to have gone through everything i have
while everyone around me believes
i'm the best i've ever been
is shattering

but only for me
because i don't let them in to see
all the broken parts of me

—**my greatest act**

i hope
i'm at least
your favorite
  mistake

our history
will keep
you and me
bonded
for eternity

you made me feel
like everything
like i was the only thing
   you could see
like everything you'd ever wanted
   was me

i still can't get over how
you made me feel that way
then let me go
and moved on

like i was never a single drop
   of anything

you broke my heart
but not in a cruel way

you were so nice
and gentle
and caring
and there for me
every step of the way

it's hard to hate you
   when all you did
was love me even after
   all the pain
you caused me

or so i thought

they feel so deep
they're so unique
these memories don't live in my head
   they're on my skin instead

i close my eyes
and feel your breath
   on my thighs

these are my favorite
moments in life

until i wake up
and turn to see
nothing but emptiness
staring at me

i can't tell the difference
   between now and then
so i'll just lie here and pretend
   you're here with me
till the end

i'm preparing myself
  for you to leave
again

while still waiting
for you to
  come back

the palm trees are swaying
the birds are chirping
the clouds are crawling
the moon is glowing
the sun is going

i am sitting
  pausing
taking in the things
  i forget exist

appreciating earth's
beautiful gifts

i just want
to feel
your body
with mine

one last time

no importaba lo que yo quería
  ise todo lo que tu deseabas
para que te quedaras
y todavía te fuiste

¿que isé mal?
¿todo no fue suficiente?

it didn't matter what i wanted
i did everything you desired
so you would stay
and still you left

what did i do wrong?
everything wasn't enough?

part one

it's been over a year
since the last time our souls connected
   i've tried many times since then
but you always rejected

finally this time
you reciprocated
and all the butterflies that were once lost
found their way back to my body
through our long overdue act of love
along with the emotions
i've denied for so long
and have gone to war with myself
to try to get rid of

in the moment
it was worth every bit
   of everything i am
but now that it's all over
the only thing i can think about
is how many steps we took back

i'm not sure where we stand
but it's a familiar place
and i just really want to go back

   —waiting for you to talk to me

i know
i deserve better
and still
i would settle
for you

why?

be my riptide
   pull me under you

we never talk about how we're really doing
what we're really feeling
we've learned to talk about the things that are nice
and keep the ones that are not
tucked deep inside us

we've learned to smile and pretend
to not show uncomfortable emotions
and dissolve vulnerability

we never address the elephants in the room
those conversations are taboo
and you wonder why we're so distant
maybe because you don't care to listen
you only hear what you want to
and ignore what would require empathy

you can only handle what's fake and easy

i hope
your heart yearns
for me
at the sound of my name

as does mine
for you
with yours

they are not coincidences
   they are signs
they are all meant to be
for reasons
you will see

pretending is easy
when you've done it long enough

eventually you'll forget you're even pretending
   and believe it's who you truly are

   —second nature

my heart
you play with
  as do i

by allowing you to break it
and coming up with every excuse why
  you are not at fault
for the emptiness that bleeds out

i hurry to pick up my broken pieces
and rush to put them back together
so i can wait for you to return
  and continue this cycle

　　—as do i

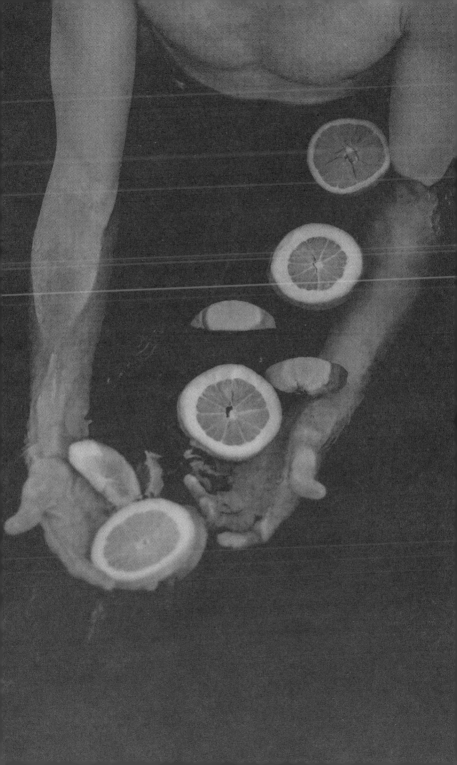

i searched more
for your love
than love for
myself

i still question if you actually cared
how much i was hurting
and how broken you made me
   you seemed to care so much
but i can't discern if all of that was true

was it all manipulation
to make yourself out to be a caring person?
was it all a part of your plan
to make me believe
everything you did to me was good-hearted?

i just can't look back at our history
and believe you didn't know
how painful it would be for me

either way you're good
   at making me believe
you're the most perfect person
   i will ever see

you possess
most of my mind

that comes with a price
and i'm the one paying it

—**forever in debt**

my favorite times
were spent with you

i hope they are
your favorite too

i want your love to flood over me

i want each raindrop to be a kiss you've given me

i want your voice screaming my name to start a hurricane

i want the waves to crash on top of me like your body

i want my heart rate rising like the tide

i want to ride you like a never-ending wave

i want to be covered in you as if i came out of the ocean

   i want you to drown me in your love

i want to drown

in you

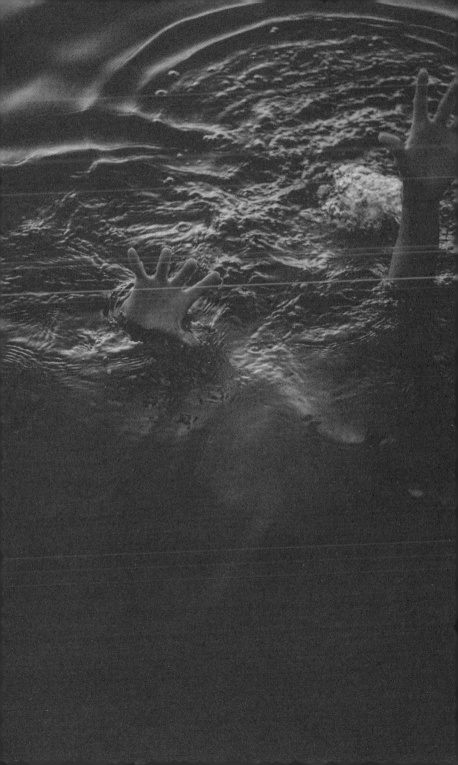

they told me one thing
  i feel another

now i battle
a constant war
over what's the truth

the sudden death
  of your love
is what killed me

going all the way
isn't always
what i seek

sometimes
i just want to lie
in bed
with your arms
wrapped around me

it's not that
i don't like you
you're just
not my type

that's okay
i guess

me voy a dormir feliz
sabiendo que estas a mi lado

besandome
amandome

por lo menos
en mi sueño

in my dream
at least

loving me
kissing me

knowing you're by my side
i go to sleep happy

i put your validation first
and my happiness second
i'm over living for your approval
and suppressing my truth

i am not this picture-perfect person
i've made myself out to be
i've lived a life that pleases you

i show you the things that make you proud
but behind closed doors
you don't know what comes out

my success is not determined by your definition
    but by my own
i hope all of my achievements
    and what makes you proud
don't get thrown out
once you know what i'm truly about

i hope i'm still the angel
you've always known me to be

i hope you'll be happy for me
to finally be
free

i always regret touching you

your skin never fails
to bring up
all the feelings
i've worked so hard to bury

every time we're side by side
i go back and forth in my mind
convincing myself
it's worth one more time
to feel my heart race
pressed against your chest
while i control my breath
and satisfy my daily fantasy

until it's over
and i feel stupid

again

don't cry
is the worst thing
you can tell someone who is hurting

make
let it all out
a habit

it's not what we did
    that felt good
it's how i felt about you
    that made it good

you've taught me to
  cherish every *i love you*
you've taught me to
  soak in every hug
you've taught me to
  treasure every smile
  and enjoy every laugh

you've taught me to
  appreciate the little things
  one day we will miss
  the most

i go out seeking
　the feeling
that ran through me
because of you
but all i find
is a feeling half full

something's always missing
　that something
is always
you

i was only good enough for you
in secret

i'll keep starving my heart
and try to convince it
all it needs to be full
is your skin

i was being who you wanted to see
not who i wanted to be

at 8:20 p.m.
you texted me
hey cutie
and my entire being
melted

you are not
responsible
for their
perception

i don't know
if what we had
was true love

but i know
it's the closest
i've ever gotten

we only talk when we need to

it's mostly about money

that seems to be your most popular and favorite topic

it became clear

when i shared that i was seeing a therapist

you didn't say a word

you didn't need to

your look spoke for you

and i responded

don't worry

the insurance covers it

again not a single word escaped your lips

but the blatant look of relief on your face

gave me all the reassurance i needed to know how much you truly cared

as i sat next to you

every ounce of my being was on its knees pleading for you to say one simple word:

why

so i could tell you why i was so broken and needed fixing

and again, that moment we shared

reminded me

you are one of the reasons

i am so broken

i only feel like this when i'm with you
i can't bear the withdrawals when you leave my side
i can't stop craving you
itching for your touch
desperately longing for you to come back
  and fill me up
with the only drug i want to feel
  running through my blood

   —addicted to you

todo lo que me dijeron de ti

fue correcto

y en vez de irme

  corriendo

me quede

para ver si ojalá

cambiabas nuestro

pensamiento

    —nunca paso

—it never happened

minds

you'd change our

to see if hopefully

i stayed

running

and instead of leaving

was true

everything they told me about you

split a piece of an escape
   took me to a place
i wish i hadn't gone

made me realize
everything that was wrong
inside me
in me deep

hidden away
and covered with cobwebs
were feelings
i didn't know owned space in me

they made themselves known
   through an experience
that was supposed to be fun
   until i was gone

they were all about love
a love i'm scared to have
a love i believe i do not deserve
i don't want to be vulnerable with anyone
forever is scary
especially tied to a significant other

what if commitment isn't for me?
why would anyone want me for more than just one night?

—another thing to talk about in therapy

how are you so good? you haven't done this before.

who says i haven't
  in my dreams

you blame your mistakes and failures
on the way you were brought up
you try to convince yourself
that your daddy issues are the reason
you're so messed up

you say your childhood trauma is what's at fault
but the choices you made as an adult
were made solely by you
not by the two who caused your so-called hurt

your feelings are valid, yes
but there comes a time
when you can either
use your past to pave your way to success
   or resent those who tried their best
and blame them for your mess

part two

it's been 29 hours since you texted me
that you don't feel good about our moment of intimacy
and that you need some time to process what happened that night

that's totally fine, i completely understand
please take your time

you must feel so confused
you must not know what to do with these intense emotions
stirred up by our special moment of love

lucky for you this all must feel new
because it's been almost two years since the last time
you felt your skin on mine
you must've forgotten our chemistry since you've been so busy
fulfilling other people's needs
   romantically

but not me i still remember unfortunately

believe me when i say
i know exactly what you're going through
everything you're feeling i've felt this entire time
ever since the day you said you wanted to end things
and just be friendly

i hope you're finally getting a taste
of all the things i still struggle with today

   —waiting for you to talk to me

i don't know
and that's okay

no tengas miedo
  yo te entiendo
y te quiero
si nomás me quisieras
en todas las mismas maneras
  que yo siempre te he querido
  seríamos algo tan tierno
tan bello
  un amor
más grande que este universo
  y más

mucho mucho más

    —**dejate amarme**

    —let yourself love me

much much more

and more
bigger than this universe
a love
so lovely
we'd be something so tender
i've always wanted you
in all of the same ways
if only you wanted me
and i want you
i understand you
don't be afraid

i took my first breath
as the me i always knew
  but was too scared to be

when i first
lay down
with you

it felt so right
  i felt so full

each second i watch you smile
while staring into the eyes
of someone who isn't me
shatters everything i'm made of

all while i suppress my true emotions
and emit a false energy
to keep you
happy

i want you next to me
  in my passenger seat
driving down long streets
fog as intense as our chemistry
chilled air blowing our hair
music caressing our ears

my hand walking up and down your thigh
you tell me all the reasons why
you wouldn't want to be anywhere else
on this cold winter night
than here next to me

—in my passenger seat

during the day
i suppress my thoughts
  of you
but at night
there's nothing i can do
  to stop myself
from dreaming
  of you

was i dumb to think
our *i love you*'s
meant the same thing?

you didn't break my heart
the idea of you did

whose fault is that?
only mine

i knew it would
end like this
still
i chose to fantasize
about what we could be
instead of listening
and letting you
go

i wanted the pain
  later
rather than
now

dancing flames inside a jar
  exhaling a perfumed scent
crisp air flowing in from outside
  brushing the hairs on my skin
crickets singing through the night

all happening while i type
all my feelings
all my thoughts
  into a word doc

releasing everything i feel
to gain freedom
from the emotions
  i carry day to day

this is my therapy
this is what saved me

—**poetry**

does your heart race
when our skins kiss?

i want you to be
what i see
first thing
every morning

i die every time
  i lie with you

you're so good
you kill me
with every one of
your moves

i live to die beneath you

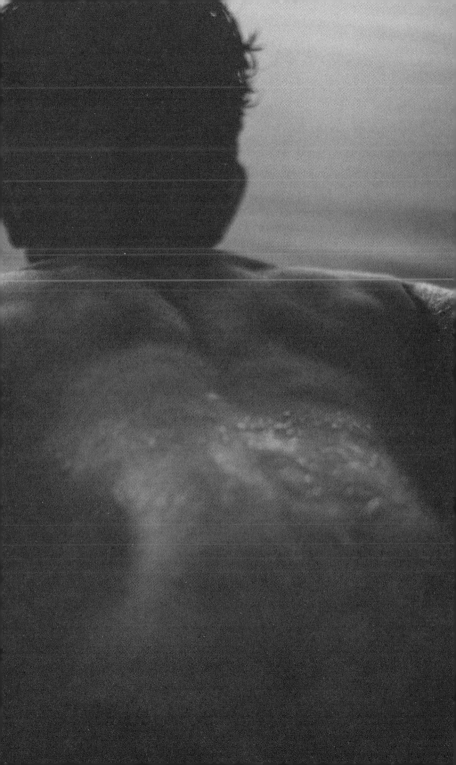

i stepped through the door of that party as everyone stared
i looked around to see who i knew
my eyes stopped when they landed on you
the smile on your face and the way you gazed
   gave me the confidence to approach you
we talked, we laughed, we flirted, we had a special kind of fun
  it was all too easy
but that didn't stop me
during the fun we took some photos on my phone
and suddenly you were more focused on me sending you those
   than continuing what we had going on
i asked *why do you want them so bad?*
you giggled and responded *i wanna see if i look cute*
do you really think i'm that dumb?
  after fixing yourself up
   you walked out and left the party with your friend
i left with the photos, a million regrets, and a few souvenirs on my neck
 all i could think about was
   would you still have done that if you didn't know who i was?
   would you still have called me cute if i wasn't on a show?
   is just me not good enough?
  i knew what the answer was
but it would hurt too much to accept that i was used
and that
   was my official welcome
   to the rest of my life

ew.

—just another hometown party

you didn't have a heart
so you took mine

without asking

i can never listen to that song
without thinking of you

i don't know
if i love or hate that

maybe both
and you

a part of me hopes
something will ignite
within you
when you see me
with someone new

i hope it makes you realize
   the treasure that i am

i hope the feelings
you never had for me
   suddenly appear
and make you wish
you were the one
on my lips

i hope you crave me
and ache from knowing
   you'll never have
another taste of me
because i found
someone new
someone who loves me
   while they have me

and shows it
as i do

there
is
more
of
me
for
me
to
see

i didn't do it for me
    i did it for you

and that
was my first
mistake

i'm tired

i'm tired of you making me feel so empty
i'm tired of wanting us in a way we will never be
i'm tired of protecting your heart while breaking mine
i'm tired of longing for you when all you do is look past me
i'm tired of my chest feeling so heavy
i'm tired of hiding how much you're hurting me
   because i want you to think i'm over the pain you've caused me
   so you can use me and not feel guilty

i'm tired

destrozado

mi corazón

por tu falta

de comunicar

tu intención

—me hubieras dicho desde el principio

—you should have told me from the beginning

your intention

of communicating

from your lack

my heart

destroyed

they say
they always come back
and you did

but for how long?

you overflow with melatonin
  when you're with me

you pretend you're listening
but all i see
is an out-of-love human
  staring at me

sometimes
the best thing you can do
is not say anything
and just listen

your empathy is felt not heard

there is comfort in silence
and love in understanding

a truthful presence
is better than a thousand
generic phrases

let's wake up
without a thing
  keeping me from
feeling your heartbeat

i want to spend the day
exploring your landscape

put your hands all over my body
treat me like a piece of meat
don't be afraid to sink
your canine teeth
into every single part
of me

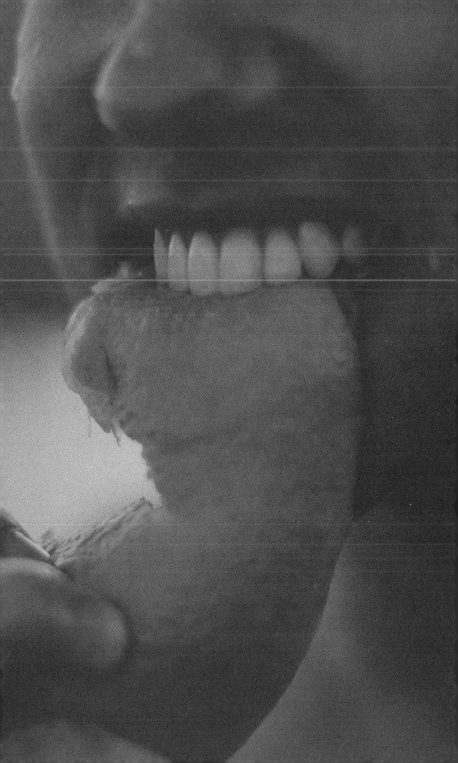

as soon as i started
forgetting you
you gave me a reason to keep
thinking of you
of us

all that work to leave you behind
to forget about what we could never be
  was for what?
just so you could come back
so easily
and make me throw it all away

you love reminding me
how much i want you
and wish you would
stay

you
make
these
tears
bleed
fierce

i feel the furthest
i've ever been
from god

but the closest
i've ever been
to my true self

what does that tell me?

i still don't know exactly
but i will
when i'm meant to

i can't wait
to think of you
and not feel pain

i fell in love with you
only because
you allowed me to

—**you led me on**

validation is prison

fui tu cielo

tu sol

tu luna

y todas las estrellas

pero nunca

tomaste un momento

para mirar hacia arriba

no sabías

  la magia

que te perdias

you were missing out on

the magic

you didn't know

to look up

took a moment

but you never

and all the stars

your moon

your sun

i was your sky

we lie restless
waiting for the world to turn on
so we can go back out
and refill our hearts
with the things that turn them
upside down

until we reunite
and bring our broken pieces together
to feel a moment
of wholeness
through our favorite motions

when i hugged you
goodbye
and walked away
my body left yours

  but my heart
stayed

just as your happiness ended
so will this pain

everything is only for a moment.

you still seek me
you still want me
in a way like we used to be
but you don't want me
completely
just a part of me

you want me
but not the commitment
of being with me
fully
so you trap me in these games
   i always fall for

convincing me to be with you
and give you what you want
of me
without you carrying the responsibility
of exclusivity

i follow your lead
because i want any part of you
   i can touch

i want more of you than just
thoughts
even though it's tearing me apart

   the moments i feel your skin
are the only moments
   i want to live in

part three

it's now been 60 hours since your text the morning after
   our little play date

i decided to reach out to ask if you were free and ready to meet
so we could discuss the things that have been eating at me

you responded
   luckily
but your response was nowhere near what i wanted to hear

you said you needed more time
   to process the intricacies
of the minutes we spent fulfilling our needs

as soon as i read those words
i felt the last bit of strength in my chest
plummet into the deepest part of my stomach

i know i have to understand that you need more time
   but these past 60 hours have felt like weeks
all this waiting is killing me

i hate this feeling more than anything
i hate not knowing what you did yesterday and the day before
i miss your morning facetimes and your knock on my door

i miss not having you in all the ways i did before
when you're ready but please hurry

   —waiting for you to talk to me

i've been trying to
get over you
for so long

it feels like
this is the only life
i've ever known

i can't wait to be reborn
  into a new life
where my heart doesn't ache
for the mediocre love
that you gave

i dreamed endlessly about you
but it didn't come true

therefore you were never a dream
for dreams do come true

—**my greatest nightmare**

your love is the best
   the highest of all
the most intense

but only because
   you're my first

maybe i wasn't the one
you wanted
but what if i was the one
you needed?

 —**now we'll never know**

this is me
until i can be
the part of me
you cannot see

i won't be free
until i let myself be
every part of me
for everyone to see

i bled
a waterfall
of feelings
for you

i wish
i could cut open my chest
dig my hand in
tear out every piece
you've broken in me
stab you with each piece
individually
and make you feel
all the pain
you've caused me
since the moment
you left me

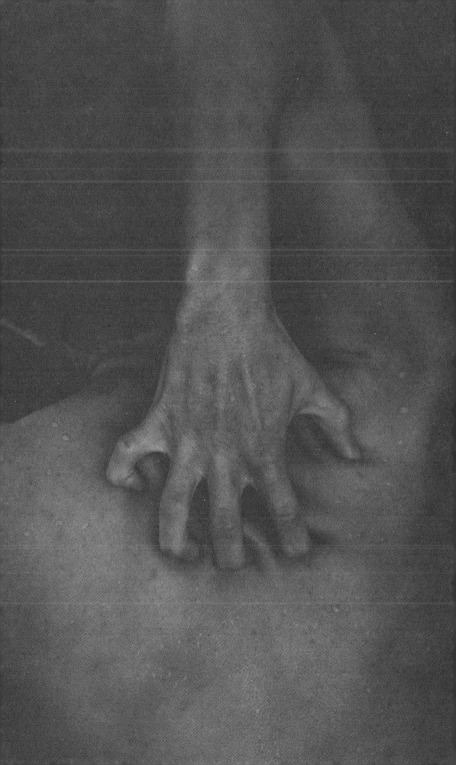

sometimes
i don't know
if i'm killing myself
or living life to the fullest

the simple thought
of your touch
gives me butterflies

our love was like something from a movie
a love i thought could never exist in real life
   only on a screen or in a book
but you taught me a fairy-tale love story can exist
when you find someone you can undress your vulnerability with
and be unapologetically you, together

it all happens so easily
once you find that person
made to be a part of
your fairy-tale dream

i just forgot every story has an end
   and not all live happily ever after

ours was only a preview of what's to come
because i'm meant for a bigger and better one
one that will go on forever
one that will end with nothing but love

and you are not in that one.

   —my fairy tale

the more you didn't want me
the harder i tried

the harder i tried
the more you didn't want me

i sit and stare at you
intently listening to the words escaping your lips
processing each sentence
absorbing every one of your emotions
transmitting my deepest empathy
telling you the things you want and need to hear
you take it all in and tell me
thank you for listening
i nod and respond
of course

i sit and stare at you
waiting to hear three simple words:
how are you
but they never come
instead you go on and on
telling me more and more about you

because in this world
the only one who exists
is you

—i sit and stare at you

i hope my smile
is the one you can't get out of your head
along with my touch
the sound of my voice saying your name
and the way my lips kissed
all your favorite places

even after
all the pain
i'll never regret
giving my
everything
to you

did you mean
everything you said
while we were
tangled up in bed?

or was it all
for fun
to help you
stay turned on?

nunca te
olvidaras de mi

no importa cuanta
gente conozcas
siempre seré
parte de tu historia

ojalá uno de
tus capítulos favoritos

your favorite chapters
hopefully one of

part of your story
i'll always be
people you meet
no matter how many

forget about me
you'll never

i gave all my love
  to you

including the piece that was
  for me

my confidence
goes down the drain
when the ones i want
look the other way

drinking my favorite liquor
until i realize who you truly are
until there's no going back
to who i thought you were

i'm crying because i thought
i finally figured out who you are
but it all disappeared once i
drank my favorite liquor
and realized how deceiving you really are

during our entire sequence
of being each other's person
    you forgot to mention
how you're seeing someone
who still to this day doesn't know
about all our special interactions

you led me to believe
    there was space for me

when in reality
i was just another convenient
piece of meat

   —no longer my favorite liquor

i want your body
   to replace these pillows on my bed
i want my head to rest on your chest
   while my soul intertwines with yours
i want to trace my fingertips along your skin
   while we tell each other about our day

i just want to love you
   in all the ways
no one else ever could

is that too much to ask?

as hard as it is to say no
the best gift you can give yourself
is walking away from a knock at the door

you've worked so hard to get to where you are
don't throw away all your progress
for another moment in their arms

keep that door locked and stand your ground
you are in control of what goes in and out

let your healing be your priority
let them see how great you're doing
without their selfish intimacy

focus on the power you feel
    from saying no

you are strong

you are beautiful

and you deserve
so much more.

if i could change the outside of me
to be everything you want to see
i would

but i can't.

why can't what's on the inside
be enough
to make you want me?

your existence is essential

how can i
expect you
to reciprocate
when your feelings
  for me
aren't the same?

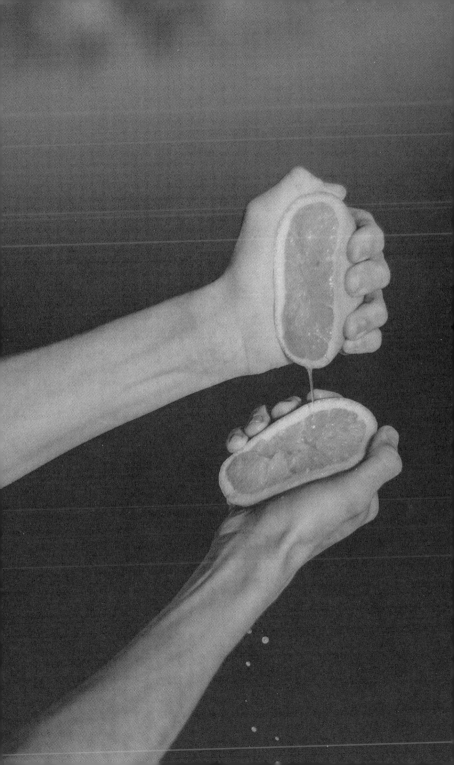

i think it's wrong
  i feel it's right

i dream of the day
you'll come running back to me
and tell me all the things
i've been running through my mind endlessly

tell me i am the one
tell me you were wrong all along
tell me you can't go on without me by your side
   because i am the one who keeps you from sleeping at night

i'll drop everything once i hear those words
jump into your arms
   and finally
call you mine

for eternity.

you changed
  my life
while being
a stranger

i can't imagine
who i'd be
if i met you

i not only
  lost you
but a part
  of me
too

you tell me
do it like this
and i do

the best teacher
showing me
how to move

you don't do it
so i fantasize it

part four

i had therapy today, two days early
my appointment is usually on fridays but i asked to be scheduled sooner
because i couldn't take another day questioning the mistakes i made
when we connected in my favorite way

i was exhausted from the constant anxiety filling my body
i hoped fifty minutes with a professional would give me an ounce of clarity
on why you would need so much time to process something
we used to do consistently

but i woke up feeling different today, everything changed in my mind
i saw our situation through a new pair of eyes

i realized what we went through was never fair to me
it only ever favored you
you always ran the show, had me when you wanted me and i never said no

i was so naïve, infatuated with the idea of finding my one, of being in love
you knew since the first time i went on top of you that we would never be
anything and still you let it happen knowing i had never done those things
that don't involve clothing

i always made excuses for you, never let myself believe you could do something
to hurt me but you did many things many times for many months

i never felt anger towards you, only myself, and now after this awakening
all i'm left with is resentment for every time you put your lips on mine
and told me that you loved me, knowing there would never be space for me
in the long run, only for the short moments you needed me
to help you reach your peak as i descended deeper into my rock bottom
without even knowing that was where i was going

    —i don't want to talk to you

you gave me clarity
on so many things
i've been questioning
for far too long

they were all the things
i hoped i wouldn't hear
   but all the things
i needed to know
   to finally
let you go

a part of me held on
to the tiniest bit of faith
that maybe
your feelings for me
would be the same

but i knew
i couldn't count on that
since you never
gave me a reason
   to believe
i was worth a shot
   to be everything
you've ever dreamed

   —secretly i knew; i always did

i want to feel your skin touching mine

while i sleep at night

your fingers running through my hair

while you stare

at me lying next to you

remembering all the reasons

you chose to spend the rest of your life

next to me

as you smile knowing

you are blessed

to have me

what hurt more
than you
leaving
was seeing
  how easy
it was
for you

this feeling will expire
  this feeling will expire
  this feeling will expire
  this feeling will expire
  this feeling will expire
this feeling will expire
this feeling will expire
  this feeling will expire
  this feeling will expire
this feeling will expire
  this feeling will expire
  this feeling will expire
this feeling will expire
this feeling will expire
this feeling will expire

this.
feeling.
will.
expire.

i hate that you know i caught feelings for you
i hate that you know our time together meant everything to me
   i hate that you know i crumbled when you cut off our intimacy
i hate that you know i go to therapy to help heal the pain you caused me
i hate that you know this book is mostly about my experience with you

so many things i hate
about our intricate relationship

but i'll never hate you
only the things you put me through

   —i hate that you know i love you

all i can do
is hope
that you felt
just a drop
of what i did
for you
and with that
   i can live

these feelings are mixed

but not forever
each in their time
will lose their power
and just be
distant
memories

for now
i'll just

feel.

fin

gracias

te amo

— abraham rodriguez

Abraham Rodriguez is an actor, poet, and artist living in Los Angeles.

Abraham discovered his passion for poetry after struggling with difficult emotions from his first broken heart. He uses poetry to help him release and better understand his thoughts and feelings.

In his debut poetry collection, *mixed feelings*, he writes about his back-and-forth sensations of love and pain from his first experience of falling in love, enduring heartbreak, and healing.

credits

creative direction: Abraham Rodriguez

editing & proofreading: Jessica Peirce

photography: Evan Murphy

cover design & interior illustrations: Andress Belk

interior design: Michelle Halket

spanish proofreading: Laura Monteverde DeWalt

publisher: Central Avenue Publishing

sales & distribution: IPG

foreign, film & audio rights: Linda Migalti,
Susan Schulman Literary Agency